NATURE UNLEASHED
VOLCANIC ERUPTIONS

Louise and Richard Spilsbury

FRANKLIN·WATTS
LONDON·SYDNEY

Franklin Watts
First published in Great Britain in 2016 by The Watts Publishing Group

Credits
Series Editors: Sarah Eason and Harriet McGregor
Series Designer: Simon Borrough
Picture Researcher: Rachel Blount

Picture credits: Cover: Shutterstock: Fotos593 (bottom), Viktoriya (right); Inside:
William Rose 13; Shutterstock: Alexey Arkhipov 15, Beboy 4–5, Bikeriderlondon
17, Alfredo Cerra 4, Crobard 21, Ecco3d 19, NoPainNoGain 7, Byelikova Oksana 23,
Photovolcanica.com 1, Volker Rauch 25, Wead 6–7; Wikimedia Commons: Jialiang
Gao (peace-on-earth.org) 27, U.S. Geological Survey Photograph / Richard P.
Hoblitt 11, Stephan Schulz 9.

HB ISBN: 978 1 4451 5259 2

Printed in China

MIX
Paper from
responsible sources
FSC® C104740

Franklin Watts
An imprint of
Hachette Children's Group
Part of The Watts Publishing Group
Carmelite House
50 Victoria Embankment
London EC4Y 0DZ

An Hachette UK Company
www.hachette.co.uk

www.franklinwatts.co.uk

Contents

VOLCANO DANGER

An erupting volcano can be spectacular but dangerous. Poisonous gas, hot ash and molten rocks spill from a hole or crack in the ground. The hot, liquid rock is called lava. As it flows down the sides of the volcano, it cools to form solid, black rock. An erupting volcano is an active volcano.

Types of Volcanoes

Some active volcanoes erupt gently most of the time. Others only erupt occasionally and they are usually more violent and dangerous. Mount Vesuvius, in Italy (see pages 14–15), is an active volcano that is likely to erupt in the near future. When Vesuvius erupted in CE 79, thousands of people in the nearby Roman city of Pompeii died. A **dormant** volcano is one that has not erupted for hundreds or even thousands of years. It is quiet now, but it may erupt in the future. An **extinct** volcano is the safest type of volcano, because it will never erupt again.

This is a plaster cast of the body of a person who was encased by molten volcanic rock that solidified as it cooled.

Measuring Disaster

Hundreds of small earthquakes are caused as **magma** rises up through cracks in the Earth's **crust**.

→ **Seismometers** are used to detect earthquakes.

Temperatures around the volcano rise as activity increases.

→ **Thermal imaging** techniques and **satellite** cameras can be used to detect heat around a volcano.

When a volcano is close to erupting it starts to release gases. The higher the sulphur content of these gases, the closer the volcano is to erupting.

→ Gas samples may be taken and **chemical sensors** used to measure sulphur levels.

Natural disasters have taken place since the Earth was formed. People have many ways of deciding what the world's worst natural disasters have been, from the deadliest disaster to the costliest. This book includes some of the worst volcanic disasters in history.

VOLCANOES IN ACTION

How does red-hot magma from deep inside the Earth explode through the Earth's surface as a volcano? Volcanoes happen because of the way the Earth is made.

Layers of the Earth

The Earth has three main layers. The **core**, or centre, is a ball of solid metal. This is the hottest part of the planet. The **mantle**, above the core, is the widest section of the Earth and consists of the partly melted rock we call magma. Magma is very hot: between 700 and 1,300 degrees Celsius (°C). We live on the crust, a thin layer of solid rock at the surface. The crust is split into large pieces called **tectonic plates**. These plates fit together like a jigsaw puzzle and float on the mantle beneath them. Volcanoes usually form in two types of places. The first is where tectonic plates meet, the second is where the magma beneath the Earth's crust is extra hot.

After many eruptions, lava cools, hardens and builds up around the opening in the crust, forming **cone**-shaped volcanic mountains.

How Volcanic Eruptions Happen

3. When magma comes out of a volcano, it is called lava.

The sides of a volcano are called a cone.

Vent

2. **Pressure** from the solid rock around the magma forces it up to the surface until magma, gas and ash explode from an opening called the central vent.

1. Magma squeezes through gaps in tectonic plates and collects below the crust.

10 MOUNT ST HELENS

By 1980, the Mount St Helens volcano in the Cascades Mountains in the state of Washington, in the United States, had been dormant, or asleep, for more than 120 years. Then at 8.32 a.m. on 18 May it erupted in an event that became the worst volcanic disaster ever in North America.

• Spokane

UNITED STATES

Mount St Helens

Deafening Disaster

The eruption turned a beautiful mountain covered in forest into a grey, empty wilderness. A total of 57 people and thousands of animals, including deer, elk and bears, were killed. Clearing up the event cost the country more than one billion dollars (£750,000). Experts had predicted a violent eruption would take place here, and they were right.

On the Record

The eruption blew off a 396-metre (m) section of the north side of the volcano. It slid down the mountain and covered a huge area of land below.

Volcanic gases exploded from the side of the volcano in a **lateral blast**. This blast travelled at speeds of 1,078 kilometres per hour (kph). It destroyed everything in its path up to a distance of 13 kilometres (km).

Mount St Helens' volcanic cone was totally blasted away by the 1980 eruption.

Between 13 km and about 21 km away, the blast flattened trees as though they were little more than toothpicks.

The eruption caused mudflows, **pyroclastic flows** and floods. Valleys up to 27 km away were covered in deep mud and **debris**.

The eruption spat out a column of gas and ash 26 km high. Some of this ash blew over 1,000 km away. The ash cloaked Spokane, Washington, about 400 km from the volcano, in total darkness.

9 MOUNT PINATUBO

By the early months of 1991 the Mount Pinatubo volcano on the island of Luzon in the Philippines had been dormant for more than 500 years. But, on 15 June 1991 it exploded in one of the world's most devastating eruptions.

Mount Pinatubo → Luzon

PHILIPPINES

Evacuation

In 1990 a huge earthquake occurred 100 km north-east of Pinatubo. **Volcanologists** started to study the volcano. By 12 June 1991, as further earthquakes and small explosions continued, they warned the 58,000 people living within 30 km of the volcano to **evacuate**. They escaped just in time.

On the Record

The cloud of ash from Mount Pinatubo turned day into night over central Luzon.

Mount Pinatubo ejected more than 4 **cubic kilometres** (cu km) of volcanic materials into the air. This created a massive cloud that rose 35 km into the air. It grew to more than 480 km across.

Within hours of the eruption, heavy rains began to wash volcanic ash and debris from the slopes onto the surrounding lowlands. This caused giant, fast-moving mudflows. About 300 people still in the area were killed when these flows flattened their houses, and 100,000 people lost their homes.

Almost 18.1 million tonnes of sulphuric ash were blasted into the **atmosphere**. The ash spread around the world in just three weeks. It caused global ground temperatures to fall by 0.5 °C for two years.

8 EL CHICHÓN

In 1982 it had been so long since El Chichón, in Mexico, last erupted – in the fourteenth century – that many people thought it was extinct. However, in March and April, a series of terrible eruptions took place. They became the worst disaster in Mexico's recent history.

El Chichón

MEXICO

Death and Destruction

The volcano was not predicted to erupt, but when it did, it killed more than 1,900 people and devastated over 20,000 homes. The disaster cost Mexico over 55 million dollars (£43.2 million) because farm cattle, and coffee, cocoa and banana farms were destroyed. The eruption produced a vast cloud of gases that circled the planet for three weeks.

On the Record

On 28 March El Chichón erupted and spewed a huge cloud of gas and ash into the air. It rose 27 km into the atmosphere in less than an hour.

The eruption, which lasted two to three hours, shot out fragments of rock that dropped onto houses like bombs. Volcanic material rolled down the sides of the volcano, causing major fires.

The eruptions created a new 1-km wide, 300-m deep **crater** that now contains a shallow lake.

After the first eruption, some people who had left the area returned. But on 4 April 1982 the volcano erupted again. Pyroclastic flows of fast-moving hot gas, ash and rock travelled up to 8 km.

The ash covered 24,000 **square kilometres** (sq km) of land.

7 MOUNT VESUVIUS

ITALY

Herculaneum • Pompeii

The eruption of Mount Vesuvius, in the Bay of Naples, southern Italy in CE 79 has given us an incredible glimpse into life in those times. The violent and sudden eruption buried the nearby Roman cities of Pompeii and Herculaneum. Thick ash from the volcano kept the bodies of the victims hidden until they were dug up 1,600 years later.

Mount Vesuvius

Warning Signs

In CE 62 a large earthquake shook Pompeii. This was then followed by minor quakes, which became worse just before the eruption, as gases built up in the cone. At that time, people did not know about the connection between earthquakes and volcanoes.

On the Record

The pressure of gases and magma rising to the surface of Vesuvius pushed out the thick layer of hard lava that plugged the vent at the top of the crater.

The eruption sent a cloud of incredibly hot rock and gas into the sky. It reached a height of 30 km. This plunged the surrounding area into darkness.

Vesuvius is the only active volcano in the whole of mainland Europe, but it is not the only volcano.

The ruins of Pompeii include houses, streets, shops and amphitheatres. Today, the site is a museum and is visited by thousands of people each year.

A massive pyroclastic flow raced down the north-west slopes. It buried Herculaneum in almost 20 m of volcanic material. More rivers of rock, gas and ash flowed through Pompeii, 10 km away.

Victims died when they choked on volcanic ash and gas, were crushed by collapsing buildings or from the extreme heat produced by the pyroclastic flow.

6 SANTA MARIA

People living near the Santa Maria volcano in Guatemala had no idea what was happening when a loud rumble began, the skies grew dark and what they thought was sand began to rain down on them. The eruption of the 3,772-m-high volcano on 25 October 1902 devastated the whole region.

San Francisco

GUATEMALA

Santa Maria

COSTA RICA

Darkening Skies

Before 25 October people did not realise that earthquakes in south-west Guatemala were signals that Santa Maria would erupt. When the volcano blew, it killed more than 5,000 people, blackened the skies over Guatemala for days and destroyed most of the country's important coffee crop for that year.

On the Record

The sound of the volcano exploding was heard as far away as Costa Rica, 850 km south of Santa Maria.

The main eruption lasted for almost 20 hours and shot out a column of ash and gas that reached 28 km into the atmosphere.

Ash from the Santa Maria eruption was found as far away as San Francisco, California, in the United States.

Santa Maria has been having small eruptions almost constantly since the 1920s.

As well as ash and toxic gas, the eruption threw out lumps of hot and cold **pumice** rock. They rained down on nearby buildings.

People reported seeing lightning form in the region of the ash cloud. Today we know that charged particles in ash clouds do create lightning.

5 NEVADO DEL RUIZ

The Nevado del Ruiz volcano in Colombia, South America, had been dormant for a long time when it began to gently rumble in 1985. Even then, people still believed it was safe until, suddenly, on 13 November the volcano burst into life with catastrophic results.

Nevado del Ruiz

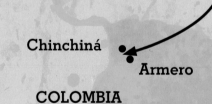

Chinchiná

Armero

COLOMBIA

Deadly Lahars

Nevado del Ruiz is 5,321 m tall, the highest of the Colombian volcanoes. There had been a deadly eruption before, in 1845, when a huge **lahar** travelled more than 70 km downstream and killed over 1,000 people.

On the Record

Nevado del Ruiz threw millions of tonnes of hot, burning ash into the air. This dropped on to and melted the snow and ice on top of the volcano, causing a mudslide.

Nevado means snow-capped. The top of Nevado del Ruiz volcano is covered in a wide area of snow and ice.

The mudslide was a mixture of mud, ash and water that was 15 m high in places. It sped down the eastern side of the volcano at 50 kph.

The mud buried four towns, including the town of Armero 48 km from the volcano. The town was buried under 5 m of mud; 23,000 of its 27,000 inhabitants died.

Mud also filled a river on the western side of the mountain, causing it to overflow. This created another mudslide that buried 1,000 people in the town of Chinchiná.

4 MOUNT PELÉE

On the morning of 8 May 1902 Mount Pelée erupted. The volcano, on the island of Martinique, destroyed the city of St Pierre, killing 30,000 people. This is the largest number of deaths caused by a volcanic eruption in the twentieth century.

Mount Pelée

MARTINIQUE

St Pierre

A Fiery Cloud

Mount Pelée is famous not only for its destructive power but also because its 1902 eruption was the first time people had witnessed and recorded the kind of pyroclastic flow it created. One survivor described the flow as a 'pit all red, like boiling, with little blue flames coming from it'. This fiery cloud of glowing gas, steam, dust, ash and pumice rock blasted down its slopes. This type of eruption is now known as 'peléan' after Mount Pelée.

On the Record

Animal behaviour indicated the first signs of trouble. Yellow ants, centipedes, snakes and other animals sensed that an eruption was coming. They began to escape down the slopes of the volcano and across nearby fields.

Before the volcano erupted, earthquakes and mudflows had killed several local people. However, there was an important election planned and politicians did not want to delay it by evacuating people.

The sand found on the beach near Mount Pelée is black because it is formed from volcanic rock.

When Pelée erupted, a giant cloud of burning gas sped down its slopes at speeds of more than 160 kph into the city of St Pierre. In minutes, the city was ruined and its inhabitants suffocated and burnt to death.

There were only two survivors in the town of St Pierre. Leon Compère Leandre, a shoemaker, escaped the burning ash in his basement. Auguste Ciparis, a convicted murderer, was protected from the heat and shock by his prison cell's stone walls.

3 KRAKATOA

When the volcano of Krakatoa, in South East Asia, erupted on 26 August 1883 the energy it released produced the loudest sound ever reported in history. The noise was so loud that people in Australia, 3,500 km away, heard it.

Krakatoa

Sumatra

INDONESIA

Java

AUSTRALIA

A Cloud of Ash

There was a series of eruptions that grew more and more violent until Krakatoa jetted out a cloud of ash and pumice rock. The energy released by the volcano was similar to that of 15,000 nuclear bombs!

On the Record

The eruptions of Krakatoa released 21 cu km of rock and sent black clouds of ash up to 80 km high above the ocean.

When the ash fell down to the ground, it covered 800,000 sq km of land. As it fell, it cloaked the area in darkness for more than two days and stopped plants from growing for five years.

Krakatoa is still active today. Local people, such as these fishermen, live and work near the volcano despite its ever-present danger.

Hawaii

After the eruption, the volcano collapsed, causing **tsunamis**, which travelled as far as Hawaii, 10,000 km away. The biggest tsunami was 37 m high. The waves battered the coasts of Java and Sumatra, killed 36,000 people and destroyed 165 coastal villages.

Gases released by Krakatoa hung in the atmosphere, blocking the sun. This caused the Earth's average temperature to drop by up to 1.2 °C. The Earth's temperatures did not return to normal until 1888.

2 SANTORINI

One of the world's worst eruptions happened in 1646 BCE on Thera, an island today known as Santorini, near Crete, in Greece. Experts are not sure whether there was one or more explosions. They do know that the eruption was devastating and may have killed 20,000 people.

GREECE

CRETE

Santorini

A Lost World

The eruptions buried a town on Thera, called Akrotiri, under a thick blanket of ash and pumice. The town remained hidden for more than 3,500 years, until workers digging out pumice to make cement found it. No bodies were found, so its inhabitants either fled in time, were buried elsewhere or were washed away by a tsunami following the eruption.

On the Record

The explosion on Thera is thought to have released as much energy as 40 nuclear bombs. It was 100 times more powerful than the eruption at Pompeii in CE 79.

During the eruption, fast-moving pyroclastic flows poured into the sea. As they hit the water, they caused enormous tsunamis that raced across the sea, hitting Crete.

Today, there are still thick layers of white pumice and black ash on the islands that make up Santorini and its neighbours.

The eruption caused pyroclastic flows of pumice. These are different to normal pyroclastic flows because they can float. They sped across the water, still burning, until they hit land.

The volcano released up to 60 cu km of magma. Scientists have found volcanic deposits up to 30 m thick at a distance of 30 km from the volcano.

On nearby Crete, thousands of people were killed by the tsunamis and pyroclastic flows.

1 MOUNT TAMBORA

The explosion of Mount Tambora in 1815 is the largest ever recorded. It ranked a seven, or 'super-colossal', on the Volcanic Explosivity Index, the second-highest rating. The volcano, which is still active, is on the island of Sumbawa in Indonesia.

Mount Tambora

INDONESIA

Java   Sumbawa

Deafening Disaster

The 1815 eruption was so loud that soldiers 1,280 km away on the island of Java were sent to fight because their leaders mistook the sound for cannon fire! Around 10,000 islanders were killed immediately as hot gas and rock sped down the mountain.

On the Record

Mount Tambora ejected about 150 cu km of ash and rock into the air.

Before it erupted, Mount Tambora was about 4,300 m high. Today it is just 2,722 m high.

The eruption of Mount Tambora left a crater 6 km across.

Pyroclastic flows raced down the slopes at more than 160 kph, all the way to the ocean 40 km away.

The eruption spewed 54.4 million tonnes of sulphur into the atmosphere.

While the death toll of people living on Sumbawa and the surrounding coastal areas was very high, even more people died after the eruption as a result of global climate change. These changes turned 1816 into 'the year without a summer' for western Europe and eastern North America, causing terrible famine. In total, the eruption caused the deaths of almost 100,000 people.

WHERE IN THE WORLD?

This map shows the locations of all the volcanic eruptions featured in this book.

Mount Vesuvius

Santorini

Mount Pinatubo

INDIAN OCEAN

Krakatoa

Mount Tambora

The area around the edge of the Pacific Ocean marks the meeting point of different tectonic plates. It is known as the 'Ring of Fire'. Looking at this map, what evidence can you see to help you explain why the area got this name?

Why do you think it is important to study volcanoes from history? How might learning about the causes and effects of eruptions in the past help save lives and property today?

Read the case studies about Mount Tambora, the number one volcano on this map, and Mount St Helens, the number ten volcano. How do they differ?

Mount St Helens

Tectonic plate boundaries

ATLANTIC OCEAN

PACIFIC OCEAN

El Chichón

Santa Maria

Mount Pelée

Nevado del Ruiz

Many deaths following a volcanic eruption are not caused directly by the volcano, but by subsequent disasters, such as tsunamis. What examples can you find in this book to support this statement?

GLOSSARY

active a volcano that could erupt at any time

ash tiny pieces of burnt rock

atmosphere the blanket of gases that surrounds the Earth

chemical sensors devices that detect chemicals present

cone the sides of a volcano

core the ball of burning-hot metal at the centre of the Earth

crater the bowl-shaped hole at the top of a volcano

crust the Earth's outer layer of solid rock

cubic kilometres volume; 1 cu km is a cube that is 1 km on each side

debris loose waste material

dormant a volcano that has not erupted for many years

evacuate get away from an area that is dangerous to somewhere that is safe

extinct a volcano that scientists do not think will erupt again

lahar a mix of water and pieces of rock that form a mudflow

lateral blast a volcanic eruption from the sides of a volcano instead of from the top

lava hot, liquid rock (called magma) when it erupts from a volcano

magma hot, liquid rock below the Earth's surface

mantle the layer inside the Earth between the crust and the core

molten melted

pressure a pushing force

pumice a very lightweight type of rock

pyroclastic flows extremely hot avalanches of gas, ash and dust; they cover everything in a thick layer of ash

satellite an object in space that travels around the Earth

seismometers machines that measure the movement of the ground during a volcano or quake

square kilometres area; 1 sq km is a square that has sides 1 km long

tectonic plates the giant pieces of rock that fit together like a jigsaw puzzle to form the Earth's crust

thermal imaging a technique that detects heat instead of light to make pictures

tsunamis huge waves

volcanologists scientists who study volcanoes

FURTHER READING

Books

Earthquakes and Volcanoes (Collins Fascinating Facts), Collins

How Hot Is Lava? (Good Question!), Kelly Smith, Sterling

Volcano and Earthquake (Eyewitness), DK Children

Websites

For fascinating clips of volcanic eruptions go to this website:
www.bbc.co.uk/science/earth/natural_disasters/volcano

For 17 explosive volcano facts visit:
www.ngkids.co.uk/science-and-nature/Volcano-Facts

Click through the links to find out about volcanic eruptions, the structure of volcanoes and how volcanoes affect us and the environment at:
www.primaryhomeworkhelp.co.uk/mountains/volcanoes.htm

Note to parents and teachers
Every effort has been made by the Publisher to ensure that these websites contain no inappropriate or offensive material. However, because of the nature of the Internet, it is impossible to guarantee that the contents of these sites will not be altered. We strongly advise that Internet access is supervised by a responsible adult.

INDEX

These are the lists of contents for each title in *Nature Unleashed:*

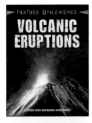

Volcanic Eruptions

Volcano Danger • Volcanoes in Action • Mount St. Helens • Pinatubo • El Chichón • Mount Vesuvius • Santa Maria • Nevado del Ruiz • Mount Pelee • Krakatau • Santorini • Mount Tambora • Where in the World? • Glossary • For More Information • Index

Earthquakes

Earthquake Danger • Earthquakes in Action • San Francisco, 1906 • Nepal, 2015 • Manjil-Rudbar, Iran, 1990 • Peru, 1970 • Kashmir, 2005 • Sichuan, 2008 • Japan, 1923 • Messina, Italy, 1908 • Tangshan, 1976 • Haiti ,2010 • Where in the World? • Glossary • For More Information • Index

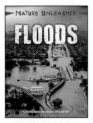

Tsunamis

Tsunami Danger • Tsunamis in Action • Flores Sea, Indonesia, 1992 • Chile, 1960 • Nankaido, Japan, 1946 • Tokaido, Japan 1923 • Papua New Guinea • San-Riku, Japan, 1933 • Andaman Sea-East Coast, 1941 • Moro Gulf, Philippines, 1976 • Japan, 2011 • Indian Ocean, 2004 • Where in the World? • Glossary • For More Information • Index

Floods

Flood Danger • Floods in Action • Mississippi Floods • Pakistan Floods, 2010 • Johnstown, 1889 • North Sea Floods, 1953 • North India Floods, 2013 • Vargas Tragedy, Venezuela, 1999 • Bangladesh, 1974 • Yangtse River Flood, 1998 • Ganges Delta, 1970 • Yellow River, China, 1931 • Where in the World? • Glossary • For More Information • Index

Hurricanes

Wind and Storm Danger • Tropical Storms in Action • Great Galveston Hurricane, 1900 • Typhoon Nina, 1975 • Hurricane Katrina, 2005 • Typhoon Bopha, 2012 • Hurricane Mitch, 1998 • Typhoon Tip, 1979 • Hurricane Camille, 1969 • Labor Day Hurricane, 1935 • Hurricane Patricia, 2015 • Typhoon Haiyan, 2013 • Where in the World? • Glossary • For More Information • Index

Wildfires

Fire Danger • Fires in Action • 2010 Russia • Ash Wednesday, 1983 • Landes Forest, 1949 • Black Saturday, 2009 • Miramichi, 1825 • Black Dragon, 1987 • Matheson Fire, 1916 • Cloquet Fire, 1918 • Peshtigo Fire, 1871 • Indonesia, 2015 • Where in the World? • Glossary • For More Information • Index